Just Enough
Difficult Topics Made Easy

Where Do Babies Come From?

Our First Talk About Birth

Dr. Jillian Roberts

illustrated by

Cindy Revell

ORCA BOOK PUBLISHERS

Library and Archives Canada Cataloguing in Publication

Roberts, Jillian, 1971–, author
Where do babies come from? : our first talk about birth /
Dr. Jillian Roberts ; illustrated by Cindy Revell.
(Just enough)

Issued in print and electronic formats.
ISBN 978-1-4598-0942-0 (bound).—ISBN 978-1-4598-0943-7 (pdf).—
ISBN 978-1-4598-0944-4 (epub)

I. Title.
QP251.5.R63 2015   j612.6   c2015-901566-9
c2015-901567-7

First published in the United States, 2015
Library of Congress Control Number: 2015934246

Summary: A nonfiction picture book that introduces very young
children to the basics of reproduction in a way that is gentle,
age-appropriate and accessible.

*Orca Book Publishers is dedicated to preserving the environment and has
printed this book on Forest Stewardship Council® certified paper.*

Orca Book Publishers gratefully acknowledges the support for
its publishing programs provided by the following agencies: the
Government of Canada through the Canada Book Fund and
the Canada Council for the Arts, and the Province of
British Columbia through the BC Arts Council
and the Book Publishing Tax Credit.

Cover and interior artwork created
digitally using Corel Painter.

Cover artwork by Cindy Revell
Design by Chantal Gabriell

ORCA BOOK PUBLISHERS
www.orcabook.com

Printed and bound in Canada.

19 18 17 16 • 5 4 3 2

This book was inspired by The Facts of Life app, a result of
the creativity, skill and hard work of students and graduates at
the Centre for Digital Media. Special thanks to Andrea Mayo,
Tom Cheung, Sheva Shen and Paula Barcante. Thanks also to
Brent Sternig and the Research Partnerships and Knowledge
Mobilization unit at the University of Victoria—and the BCIC
StartSmart voucher program—for providing significant support,
guidance and resources to expand the reach and scope of The Facts
of Life project. Without the collaboration of these amazingly
inspired teams, the project would not have been possible.
Thank you!

The Facts of Life app is available for download.

For all the children in my life—and most especially
for Lauren, Ally & Jack.

—JR

For Amanda, the dreamer and thinker, and Connal,
the guy with a can-do attitude.

—CR

Nature has given every living thing a way to make a baby.

But where do all those babies come from?

Babies come from their mothers' bodies. When a woman has
a baby growing inside of her, she is said to be *pregnant* or
expecting a baby.

What part of the mother's body does the baby come from?

A baby comes from the mother's *womb*, which is just below the stomach. It provides a safe place for the baby to grow.

How does the baby start growing in the first place?

Two ingredients are needed to make a baby. A *sperm* and an *egg*. When the sperm and the egg come together, a baby might begin to grow.

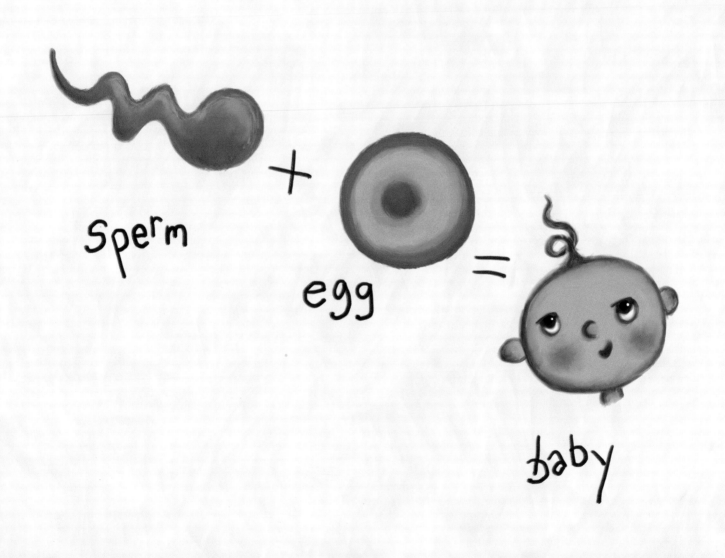

Sperm + egg = baby

Where do the baby ingredients come from?

The sperm comes from the father's body and the egg comes from the mother's body. When it's time to make a baby, these two bodies fit together. The sperm finds the egg, and a seed may be planted in the mother's womb.

That seed starts very little and grows into a big baby.

How does the baby grow?

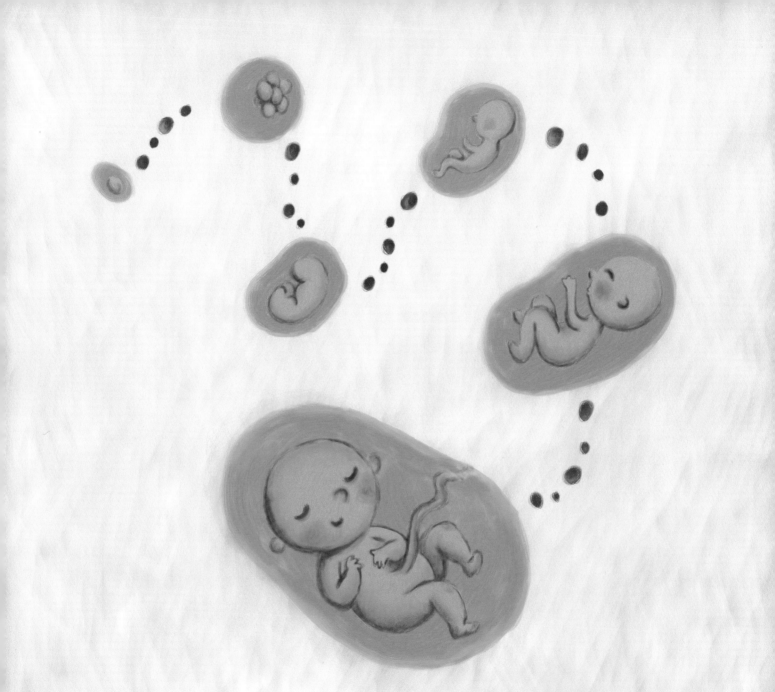

The baby grows when it's fed.

How does the baby eat?

A bit of the mother's food feeds the baby through a special tube called an *umbilical cord*. This connects the baby to its mother.

When the baby is born, the umbilical cord falls off and leaves a belly button.

Look, you have a belly button too!

How long does it take to grow a baby?

Babies usually take nine months to grow. They start out tinier than a pea and can grow to be the size of a watermelon. When the baby is fully developed, it is ready to be born.

month 1

month 2

month 3

month 4

month 5

month 6

month 7

month 8

month 9

How does the baby get out?

When it's time for the baby to be born, he or she is delivered through the mother's birth canal. A baby can be born at home or in a hospital.

Each and every one of us started life as a little seed.

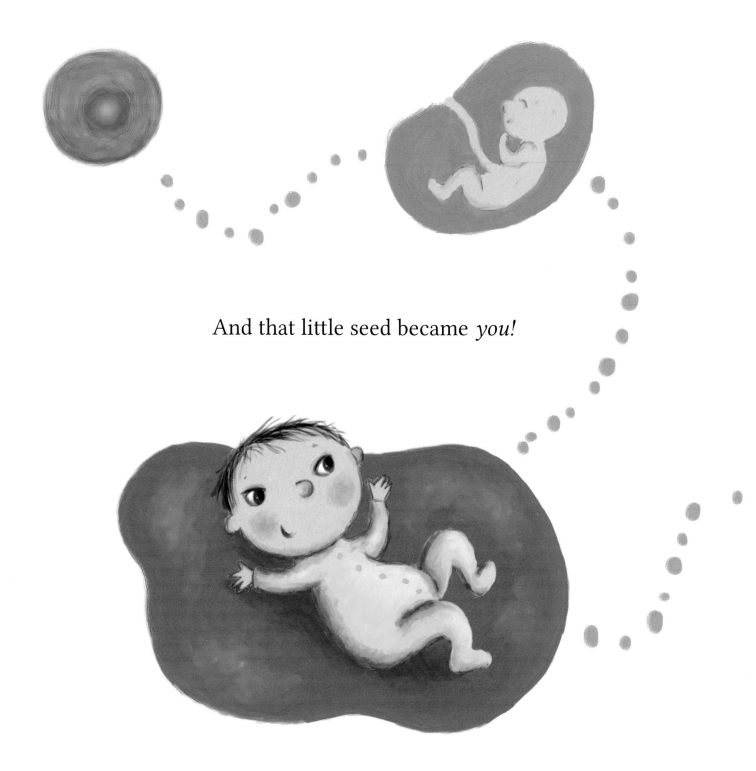

And that little seed became *you!*

Just A Few More Questions

How does the sperm find the egg?

Often when a couple wants to make a baby, the father's penis, which contains the sperm, fits inside the mother's vagina. The sperm then swims through the penis into the vagina, where it will find and fertilize the egg. But babies can be conceived in other ways too. In a process called *in vitro fertilization*, eggs and sperm are combined outside the body. Then fertilized eggs are placed back inside the mother's womb. In either case, a single fertilized egg may be the start of a brand-new baby.

Who helps bring babies into the world?

Many types of doctors and professionals can help with the conception and birth of a new baby. A fertility specialist can help bring the sperm and egg together in the beginning. Midwives are specialists who can assist the mother before, during and after birth. Sometimes a family doctor can help to deliver the baby. If a baby cannot be born through the vagina, or birth canal, an obstetrician can help the baby come out by performing a surgery called a *Cesarean section*. These are just some of the people who can provide support for those expecting a child.

What about babies who were adopted? Where do they come from?

Adopted babies come from a fertilized egg just like every other baby. Sometimes, for many different reasons, a biological mother or birth parent is unable to take care of a new baby. When this happens, the birth parent may give the baby to another family to adopt. The baby then belongs to the adopted family and is loved just as any other baby would be.

What about families with only one mom or dad? Or two moms or two dads? How do different kinds of families have babies?

Babies can be born into all shapes and sizes of families! Sometimes single parents or same-sex parents choose to have a baby on their own or with the help of a doctor. Sometimes they choose to adopt babies. No matter what size or shape a family is, a baby is always loved very, very much.